BENNETT CERF

Stories to Make
You Feel Better

Introduction by
JOHN CHARLES DALY

G.K.HALL &CO.

 Boston, Massachusetts

1973

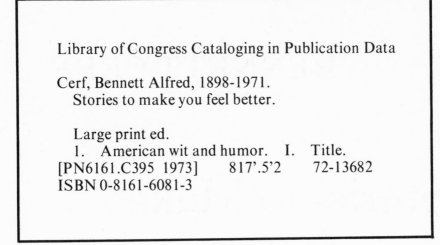

Library of Congress Cataloging in Publication Data

Cerf, Bennett Alfred, 1898-1971.
  Stories to make you feel better.

  Large print ed.
  1.   American wit and humor.   I.   Title.
[PN6161.C395 1973]   817'.5'2   72-13682
  ISBN 0-8161-6081-3

Published in Large Print by arrangement with Random House, New York

Set in Photon 18 pt. Times Roman

STORIES TO MAKE
YOU FEEL BETTER

Contents

Very Nice People

Introduction

Bennett Cerf had all the qualities of the leprechaun except, of course, there was the lean six-foot frame and the exuberant, confident clarion voice.

My Irish forebears knew the leprechauns as "the happy people," not so much because they were but because they gave happiness to others by lifting the mind and the spirit out of the dull, dreary, everyday world and transporting them into that indefinable middle estate between the reality of earth and the vision of heaven. I thought of the leprechauns as I studied a photograph on the office wall the other day. It was taken on a Sunday night, some five years ago, when CBS had a photographer roaming around backstage to get some candids for the coming season's promotion for our television show "What's My Line?" Bennett is grinning like a Cheshire cat and I am convulsed with laughter. I don't remember what he had said or done to produce my happy condition, but it's not important. At the very least, Bennett put a smile upon any day on which you were lucky enough to run into him.

I remember, at the very beginning, in 1950, there was some uncertainty in putting together the "What's My Line?" panel. On the first program Harold Hoffman, former Governor of New Jersey, Dr. Richard Hoffman, a well-known psychiatrist in New York, and Louis Untermeyer, the poet, shared the panel's responsibilities with Arlene Francis. It was several months before Bennett took his place on Sunday night. About that time, things began to settle down. A nice balance of enthusiasm, erudition and euphoria entered the scene and our Sunday nights took on that special quality which, I am sure, made Arlene Francis, Dorothy Kilgallen, Bennett and me welcome in so many homes every week for more than seventeen years.

Thinking back over the years, I realize that the old guard came to be very close friends. In a way, it's surprising, for we didn't see a great deal of one another. After the early years, we had our Sunday chores reduced to a science, spending less than an hour in the theatre—some chit-chat, a little make-up, the program and, then, we were off to our vocations—Dorothy and I to journalism, Arlene to the theatre and Bennett to Random House. Occasionally we'd gather at Cherio's, or some other place, for a nightcap, and three or four times a year we'd spend an entire evening or weekend together at Arlene's or Dorothy's or Bennett's house in the city or up in the country. And yet, as I think of the friends who have been most cherished in the passing years, Bennett comes immediately to mind.

We worked together occasionally on some boards and committees, and Bennett was always after me to write a book. He had so much energy himself, he just couldn't understand why I felt I had all I could handle running a network news department and reporting news on radio and television six days a week. To "Old Inexhaustible" there were seven days in a week, so why didn't I write a book?

On rare occasions Bennett could be brought to the boiling point, and his forthrightness would put a longshoreman to shame. But he had an overwhelming sense of the ironies of life and calmly accepted man as a less than perfect animal.

"The real excitement," he once said, "is having somebody new come along, helping him to get famous and watching him move to Hollywood and start calling me a son-of-a-bitch." Then he'd roar with laughter.

He loved his world of publishing. Courageous, shrewd, loving what was good in literature and with a keen sense of the public taste and the marketplace, he won a signal victory over government censorship in court in 1934 and published an unabridged *Ulysses,* James Joyce's masterpiece. Thirty-two years later he made a best seller out of his *Random House Dictionary of the English Language.* I suggested he had only one more world to conquer and that he must now work on making a best seller out of the New York phone book, which "Ma Bell" had been foolishly giving away. He grinned from ear to ear.

In between Joyce and the dictionary, there was Eugene O'Neill, William

Faulkner, W. H. Auden, Gertrude Stein, William Saroyan, James Michener, John O'Hara, Robert Penn Warren, Truman Capote, Robinson Jeffers, etc., etc.

By Bennett's own description, he reveled in his very own streak of pure unadulterated ham. He loved publicity and proclaimed it to the heavens. He loved his lecture tours and approached them with all of the enthusiasm of a youngster off to a birthday party. I know how grueling the lecture circuit can be and once braced him with "Dammit, you're richer than Croesus, why do you beat yourself up on the circuit?" He looked thoughtful for a moment and said, "I can't tell you what a kick I get out of it. The wonder of all those people wanting to come to hear what I have to say—and even willing to pay for it—never leaves me."

Bennett's great abilities carved out for him a permanent niche in the pantheon of publishing. But what touched and brightened our lives as the grand humanity and humor in him, the substance of which is all here in *Stories to Make You Feel Better.*

JOHN CHARLES DALY
March, 1972

5

Foreword

This little book is a collection of stories that I have chosen for two explicit purposes—one: to cheer up individuals who may be undergoing a siege of sickness or have succumbed temporarily to a prevailing mood of depression, and two: to remind those of faint heart that ninety-nine and a half percent of our fellow citizens continue to be the decent folks they always were—friendly, loyal, hopeful of the future, and willing to meet more than halfway anybody who approaches them in a similar spirit.

I'm tired—and aren't you?—of the spotlight being continuously focused in TV shows and news stories on the rotten apples in our barrel. Let's redirect our attention to the American people, young and old, who continue to be simply wonderful!

You'll meet some of them in these pages.

BENNETT CERF
August 10, 1971

7

V. N. P.*
*Very Nice People

One of the nicest stories I've heard in a long time concerns a writer who through no fault of his own lost two fine jobs in the space of a single year.

First, the magazine on which he served as managing editor folded, and then the newspaper to which he transferred was bought by an opposition syndicate, and suspended publication at once, with the casualty list embracing the entire staff.

He came home to his wife and three small sons, and told them ruefully, "I'm out of a job again. The paper stopped publishing with this evening's edition." The wife comforted him as best she could. The three boys stared at him round-eyed.

Next morning the writer arose after the boys had left for school and wandered into his study.

In the wastebasket were the remains of three china piggy banks. On the dining-room table was a pile of quarters, dimes, and nickels. There was a crudely lettered sign under the coins. I read, "We believe in you, Pop."

11

Several times a year Ed Sullivan performs a worthy service indeed. He persuades a group of top-flight Broadway stars to accompany him to Halloran General Hospital in Staten Island to entertain the sorely wounded war veterans there.

For one of these expeditions, Sullivan sought out the beloved veteran Jimmy Durante, who accepted the invitation but explained in advance that he had a very remunerative date to perform at a private party later that night and would, accordingly, be able to do only one number for the boys.

The number he chose, naturally, was his famous "Inky Dinky Doo," and at its conclusion the audience was so ecstatic that he grabbed the microphone back and did eight more complete routines.

When he finally staggered off the platform, exhausted, Sullivan cried, "You were just great, Jimmy, but didn't you see me signaling to you? What came into you? You'll never make your private party now!"

"Look at the front row of that audience," Durante told him, "and you'll see why I forgot all about that private engagement."

Ed Sullivan poked his head through the curtain and spotted two lieutenants in a first-row divan, applauding happily. The lieutenant on the right had lost his left arm; the one on the left his right arm. With no semblance of self-consciousness, they were clapping their two remaining hands together, and giving Jimmy Durante the most soul-satisfying round of applause he ever in his life had received.

During quail season in Georgia, an Atlanta journalist met an old farmer hunting with an ancient pointer at his side. Twice the dog ran rheumatically ahead and pointed. Twice his master fired into the open air. When the journalist saw no birds rise, he asked the farmer for an explanation.

"Shucks," grinned the old man. "I knew there warn't no birds in that grass. Spot's nose ain't what it used to be. But him and me have had some wonderful times together. He's still doing the best he can—and it'd be mighty mean of me to call him a liar at this stage of the game!"

If the ever-reliable (although not always coherent) Mr. Casey Stengel can be believed, Yogi Berra, peerless catcher for the New York Yankees ball club in the good old days, once performed a kind act indeed.

The team was in spring training in St. Petersburg, Florida, and Yogi was digesting his evening meal on the veranda of a hotel there, when his attention was drawn to a little girl who was playing on the deeply sloped corrugated-tin awning of a store across the road. She was teetering closer and closer to the awning's edge, and sure enough, there came the moment when she fell off.

That's when Yogi, quick as a flash, leaped to his feet, dashed across the road and caught the little girl in his arms before she hit the pavement.

Unfortunately, continues Mr. Stengel with a perfectly straight face, Yogi took the fine edge off his praiseworthy gesture when out of sheer force of habit—he threw the little girl to second base!

15

One of the elder Du Ponts of Wilmington had a collection of Ming china second to none in the world. He kept it in a little museum on his estate, and allowed occasional visitors to inspect his treasures.

A young couple was there by invitation. While waiting for their host, the girl picked up a delicate vase. To her horror, it slipped from her fingers and smashed into a hundred fragments on the stone floor. Just then little Mr. Du Pont came pattering up.

"Oh, Mr. Du Pont," wailed the girl, "I have broken the little vase that stood in this niche. I do hope it wasn't one of the valuable pieces."

Mr. Du Pont took a quick look at the broken fragments. "Fortunately, my dear," he said, with a reassuring pat, "it wasn't valuable at all. Don't trouble your pretty head about it."

Then he fainted dead away.

Heartwarming ad in the classified section of a dignified metropolitan newspaper: "I am fully responsible for all debts and obligations of my wife, Selma, both present and future, and am delighted to be the provider for a woman who has borne me two fine children, listened patiently to all my gripes, and with an overabundance of love and care, made the past fifteen years of my life the happiest I have known. On this, our fifteenth wedding anniversary, I am proud to express my gratitude publicly."

Not long ago a magazine aimed at a rural audience printed a picture of a deserted farmhouse in a desolate, sand-swept field, then offered a prize for the best hundred-word essay on the disastrous effect of land erosion. A bright Indian lad from Oklahoma bagged the trophy with this graphic contribution:

Picture show why white man crazy. Cut down trees. Make too big tepee. Wind blow soil. Grass gone. Door gone. Window gone. Squaw gone. Whole place gone to hell. No pig. No corn. No pony.

Indian no plow land. Keep grass. Buffalo eat grass. Indian eat buffalo. Hide make plenty big tepee. Make moccasin. All time eat. Indian no need hunt job. No hitchhike. No ask relief. No build dam. No give dam.

White man heap crazy.

Before Lou Little became the most successful football coach in Columbia University history, he occupied a similar post at Georgetown University. One year there was a youngster on the squad who was no great shakes as a football player, but whose personality served as a morale booster for the whole team. Little was deeply fond of the boy. He liked the proud way he walked arm-in-arm with his father on the campus from time to time. If the team was far enough ahead, Little even let him get into a game occasionally for the last few minutes of play.

One day, about a week before the big finale with Fordham, the boy's mother called Little on the phone. "My husband died this morning of a heart attack," she said. "Will you break the news to my boy? He'll take it better if it comes from you." Little did what was necessary, and the boy went home sorrowfully.

He was back three days later, and came straight to Lou Little. "Coach," he begged,

"I want to ask something of you that means an awful lot to me. I want to start on that game against Fordham. I think it's what my father would have liked most."

Little hesitated, and then agreed. "Okay, son, you'll start, but you'll only be in there for a play or two. You aren't quite good enough, and you know it." True to his word, Little started the boy—but never took him out. For sixty full, jarring minutes he played inspired football — running, blocking, and passing like an all-American, and sparking the team to victory.

Back in the clubhouse, Little threw his arm around the boy's shoulder and said, "Son, you were terrific today. You stayed in because you belonged there. You never played that kind of football before. What got into you?"

The boy answered, "Remember how my father and I used to go about arm-in-arm? There was something about him very few people knew. My father was totally blind. This afternoon was the first time he ever saw me play."

A cheerful truckdriver pulled up at a roadside tavern in the middle of the night for a spot of refreshment. Halfway through his dinner, three wild-looking motorcyclists roared up — bearded, leather-jacketed, filthy—with swastikas adorning their chests and helmets.

For no reason at all they selected the truckdriver as a target. One poured pepper over his head, another stole his apple pie, the third deliberately upset his cup of coffee. The trucker never said one word—just arose, paid his check, and exited.

"That palooka sure ain't much of a fighter," sneered one of the invaders.

The man behind the counter, peering out into the night, added, "He doesn't seem to be much of a driver either. He just ran his truck over three motorcycles!"

It was at a small dinner party honoring Howard Lindsay's birthday that the guest of honor made a very brief speech of acknowledgment that brought a tear of sheer pleasure to the eyes of everyone in the room.

Beaming at the assembled guests, Lindsay said reflectively, "There are a number of people I know that I love but, unfortunately, do not respect. There are others I respect but do not love. But here in this room with me tonight are the people in this world that I both love *and* respect." Then he sat down.

Did everybody there feel better? You just bet they did!

From Birmingham, a very nice person writes:

I could tell from the bus driver's greeting when the blind lady climbed aboard that she must be a very frequent passenger. She sat down directly behind him and they carried on an animated conversation as he drove.

When we reached the woman's stop the driver got out and escorted her through heavy traffic to the other side of the street. When he returned to his seat I noticed the woman still standing where he had left her. "She won't budge till she knows I got back safely," he explained. He honked his horn three times, the woman waved, and off we drove.

"I feel good," said the driver.

I answered, "So do I."

One of the most enchanting — and successful—comedies ever produced is Lindsay and Crouse's *Life with Father,* based on the equally irresistible book by Clarence Day. I reread it regularly about once a year and urge you to do likewise. You will find yourself chuckling happily from beginning to end.

In one heartwarming scene, wife Vinnie is coping with irascible Father at the breakfast table, breaking the news as gently as possible that the rector is coming to tea that afternoon. Father harrumphs, "I'm glad you warned me. I'll go to the club."

"I do wish," sighs Vinnie, "you'd take a little more interest in the church."

"Vinnie," counters Father, "getting me into heaven's your job. Everybody loves you so much—I'm sure God must, too."

"I'll do my best," she promises. "It wouldn't be heaven without you."

That's when Father delivers one of my favorite lines in the play—and a pure and beautiful declaration of love.

"If you're in heaven, Vinnie," he promises, "I'll manage to get in some way, even if I have to climb the fence!"

Two silver-haired old ladies rumbled down the main street of a New England town in their beaten-up coupe, made an illegal turn, and compounded their felony by ignoring the outraged traffic officer's endeavors to stop them. He finally caught up with them in front of Ye Olde Waffle Shoppe. "Didn't you hear my whistle?" he demanded angrily.

The perky octogenarian at the wheel glanced at him coyly and admitted, "Yes, I did, Officer — but I never flirt when I'm driving."

The cop looked astonished, then broke into a broad grin. "You win, lady! Drive on!"

Adlai Stevenson, who knew how to tell a good story, broke up a Long Island rally one night by recalling the prudish, tight-lipped old maid who wouldn't even allow her pet cat out of the house after dark. Headed for New York on one of her infrequent outings, she paused to remind the maid about locking up that cat each evening.

This time in New York, however, the old maid encountered a handsome old rogue who swept her off her feet. After four nights of blissful romancing, she wired her maid: "Having the time of my life. *Let the cat out!*"

There once dwelled in czarist Russia a rabbi with such a golden voice that everybody clamored to hear him. In his sleigh he made a triumphal tour. At each city he visited, pretty girls pelted him with roses and rich merchants plied him with compliments and gifts.

Outside one town, the rabbi's faithful driver stopped the sleigh and suggested, "Rabbi, for once I'd like to be the one receiving all the honors and attention. Just for tonight, change clothes with me. You be the driver and I'll be the rabbi."

The preacher, a merry and generous soul, agreed, but added, "Remember, clothes do not make the man. If you're asked to explain some difficult passage of the Talmudic laws, see that you don't make a fool of yourself."

The exchange was effected. When the two men arrived at their destination, the bogus rabbi was received with tumultuous enthusiasm, and obviously enjoyed every minute of it. Furthermore, since he had heard the rabbi's speech a hundred times, he delivered it faultlessly.

Then, however, came the dreaded

question period. Sure enough, an aged scholar arose and propounded a tricky, delicate question. The real rabbi in the back of the hall groaned, "Now he'll make a fool of himself."

But the driver was equal to the occasion. "A fine scholar you are!" he scoffed. "Why, your problem is such a simple one that even the old dull-witted fellow who drives my sleigh must know the answer. *Driver, come up here to the platform and answer this poor fellow!*"

A distressed lady came to her family counselor, declaring, "I hate my husband! I not only want to divorce him, but I want to make things as tough for him as I possibly can."

"I know just how you should proceed," the old counselor assured her. "Start showering him with compliments and indulging his every whim. Then, just when he knows how much he needs you—you start divorce proceedings. You'll fracture him!"

The wife decided this was sound advice.

Six months later the counselor met her at a dinner and asked, "Are you still following my suggestion?"

"I am," said the wife.

"Then how about filing your divorce papers?" pursued the counselor.

"Are you out of your head?" countered the wife indignantly. "We're divinely happy! I love him with all my heart!"

One of the greatest mayors New York had was Fiorello La Guardia—"The Little Flower." Every New Yorker remembers the day Fiorello read the funny papers over the radio—with all the appropriate excitement and inflections—when a strike kept the Sunday journals off the stands. They remember, too, his squeaky fulminations against the "crooks" and "tinhorns" in our town, and his weekly radio sign-off, "Patience and fortitude."

One time the ubiquitous mayor chose to preside in a night court. It was bitter cold outside. A trembling man was brought before him, charged with stealing a loaf of bread. His family, he said, was starving.

"I've got to punish you," declared La Guardia. "The law makes no exceptions. I must fine you ten dollars." But The Little Flower was reaching into his own pocket as he added, "Well, here's the ten dollars to pay your fine—which I now remit." He tossed the ten-dollar bill into his famous sombrero. "Furthermore," he declared, "I'm going to fine everybody in this courtroom fifty cents for living in a town where a man has to steal bread in order to eat. Mr. Bailiff, collect the fines and give them to this defendant!"

The hat was passed and an incredulous old man, with a light of heaven in his eyes, left the courtroom with a stake of $47.50

You've heard lots of mean stories about agents for finance companies swooping down on delinquents and repossessing autos, TV sets, pianos, and what not. Here's a nice story for a change.

An agent had to remind a nice old farmer that he hadn't paid the last two of fifty installments on a new car. "It's in the barn," said the farmer sadly—and in a low voice so his wife couldn't hear, "Sickness cost us too much this year. I'm afraid you'll have to take that car of yours back."

The agent walked reluctantly to the barn. There he was amazed to find the automobile shiny and new, up on blocks, carefully covered with a tarpaulin, with the speedometer showing only twelve miles—the distance from the auto salesroom to the farmer's barn.

"But you've never really used this car!" exclaimed the agent.

"Didn't feel I should" explained the farmer. "I figured she's not mine till she's fully paid for."

The agent slammed shut his collection book, put the tarpaulin back over the car, and said, "Pop, I guess we'll just let you have this car till your crops come in."

One sultry midsummer afternoon in mid-Manhattan, eight months after Pearl Harbor, three young soldiers and their girls, headed for Central Park, stopped involuntarily at the sound of enchanting music emanating through the open second-story windows of a handsome red-brick private home across the street. What they didn't know was that the home was owned by Jules Glaenzer, the American head of Cartier's. What they did know was that they had never heard lovelier singing in their lives.

Mr. Glaenzer noticed them standing entranced and impulsively invited them all inside. Thereupon they spread themselves on the drawing-room floor and listened to a dazzling concert of a dozen and more current song hits.

It was only after all of them had wolfed a snack dinner whipped up by Mr. Glaenzer that the six youngsters were told the identity of their entertainers. The singer was the incomparable Judy Garland (hard to recognize without her movie make-up!). Her accompanist was the famous composer Richard Rodgers!

"We're headed for the front soon," one of the soldiers confided before they left, "but we're certainly never going to forget this most wonderful and exciting afternoon of our lives." Then his face clouded. "There's just one catch," he added. "When we tell this story, who in God's name is going to believe us?"

A story I've always loved, told by Carl Sandburg in his biography of Abraham Lincoln, has for its heroine a little spindly legged nine-year-old girl named Grace Bedell, who lived in the upstate New York village of Westfield in 1860.

The first time she saw a picture of the newly elected President of the United States, she thought he would be better-looking and more impressive if he grew whiskers, and what is more, she sat down and wrote him so. Mr. Lincoln, amused, gravely replied that people might accuse him of silly affectation for sprouting a beard at this stage of his career.

No, answered Grace, it was the right thing for him to do, for he looked too solemn, and she believed other little girls, like herself, would be scared of him without whiskers.

When Mr. Lincoln's special train carried him from Illinois to New York, and then on to the inauguration in Washington, he ordered a stop at Westfield, and from the rear platform, announced, "I have a correspondent in this town named Grace Bedell, and if she's present, I hope she'll step forward."

"Here I am," called out the flabbergasted Grace.

"Well, Grace," beamed Mr. Lincoln, leaning over the rear rail, "you see, I let these whiskers grow for you! I hope you think I'm better-looking now."

"You look wonderful now," she assured him, "and I bet you're going to be the greatest President this country ever had!"

Mr. Lincoln put his stovepipe hat back on his head, the train puffed away—and maybe one or two spectators realized that they had just seen an example of American democracy really clicking on every cylinder!

Famed motion-picture producer Billy Wilder tells of the day he tried to persuade Sam Goldwyn to let him do a picture on the life of the great Russian ballet star Nijinsky. Said star unfortunately had come to a disastrous end, spending the last years of his existence in an insane asylum — convinced he was a horse.

"Now listen to me, Billy," argued Goldwyn, "if you think I'm going to invest three million dollars in a picture about a man who thinks he's a horse, you're even crazier than he is."

"We can give the story a happy ending," urged Wilder. "We'll have him win the Kentucky Derby!"

Two rather handsome gray-haired men, neatly but unostentatiously garbed, found themselves occupying the same park bench in midtown Manhattan one summer midday. In front of them towered one of New York's most famous hostelries. The man on the left smiled wistfully. "Beautiful hotel, isn't it?" he asked. "You know, I'd rather like eating a good lunch in its main dining room today. There's a slight drawback, however. I haven't a single penny in my pocket."

"That's odd," said the other. "Neither have I." A moment later he added, "Let me offer a suggestion. Both of us make a decent enough appearance. Let's pop over to that dining room and order the fanciest food and wines on the menu. Just before the check comes, we'll borrow a coin from the waiter, and toss to see who walks out a free man and who stays to face the music."

"Done and done," declared the first man promptly.

The luncheon was an unqualified success. The food was delicious, the conversation sparkling. The demitasses were already on the table when one man, after considerable hemming and hawing, said, "Look here, old man. I'm afraid I'm guilty of a bit of deception. When I told you over in the park that I didn't have a cent with me, it was God's honest truth. But please stop worrying about this lunch check. I'll take care of it. I'm worth a mint. I simply forgot to transfer my belongings when I put on my new suit this morning. Fact is, if I must confess, I occupy the most expensive suite in the place."

"I guess that makes us even," laughed the other. "I should have recognized you. I own the hotel."

A tragic moment in the life of a fading Broadway star comes when he finally must face the fact that the parade has passed him by. No longer is he offered the choice of a half-dozen fat parts at the start of the season. Stony-eyed autograph hounds gaze blankly into his face. Columnists have forgotten even how he spells his name. If he has neglected to save for this very rainy day while the cash was pouring in, the awakening is doubly painful.

One such disillusioned thespian had fallen so far from glory that he didn't know where his next month's rent was coming from, and with the Christmas season approaching, gratefully accepted the one job that was offered to him, playing Santa Claus in a big department store. He donned the traditional costume and whiskers, and with a brave attempt at joviality but with a sinking heart, climbed to his seat in the toy department.

A long line of children was waiting to be dandled on his knee and to whisper lists of all the presents they craved. One little boy was so much gayer and more charming than the rest that the actor felt a sudden surge of

41

warmth in his heart. "I'd like to have a look at your mommy," he told the boy. "Here she comes for me now" was the reply.

The actor looked up and caught his breath — he was gazing straight into the eyes of the glamorous woman who had once been his leading lady. More, she had once been his wife; but their marriage had failed years before, and he had read that she had married a respected and prosperous businessman.

Fortunately she did not appear to penetrate his disguise. "You have a fine boy here," he said, summoning all his courage to keep his voice from breaking. "He wants a space suit, a rocket ship, and an autographed picture of Captain Video."

The lady winked gravely at Santa and said, "I know you'll get them for him, won't you?"

"But, Mommy," interrupted the boy, "how will Santa Claus find me? Give him our address!"

The mother indulgently went to a nearby desk to fill out a card, which she placed in an envelope and left in Santa's hands. He sighed with relief when she disappeared down the corridor. Then he opened the envelope.

The card read, "Merry Christmas to the greatest actor I ever knew." Clipped to it was a check for one thousand dollars.

There's an eighty-two-year-old obstetrician in Bridgeport who looks like one of those memorable Normal Rockwell covers for the *Saturday Evening Post* — silvery white hair, twinkling blue eyes, ruddy cheeks, a perky bow tie — who has delivered over two thousand babies in his illustrious career. Furthermore, his charge for his invaluable services is either one hundred or two hundred dollars.

Naturally, I was curious to know how he decided which bill to submit. Did he look up the father's financial rating? "Nonsense, I couldn't care less," he assured me. "What then?" I persisted.

"It's very simple," smiled the doctor. "Every time I deliver a baby, the father is pacing nervously up and down in the waiting room. When I put my had on his shoulder and tell him, 'Congratulations! You have a beautiful new baby,' he invariably asks me one of two questions. If it's 'Is it a boy or a girl?' I charge him two hundred dollars, but if he asks 'How's my wife?' I only charge him a hundred!"

This is the story of an unfortunate little orphaned girl of twelve, ungainly defiant, ill-mannered, who had been shunted from one institution to another all her life. Now, in new surroundings, she lost no time in once more antagonizing her companions and fraying the nerves of her housemother and the head of the institution.

Everybody was praying for an opportunity to get rid of her, and one day that opportunity seemingly arrived. One of the strict rules of the asylum was that no letter could be mailed by an inmate without the approval of a teacher. It was with understandable excitement, therefore, that the little girl's housemother reported to the principal, "Her roommate has confided to me that she's been writing a note every day now for a week and hiding it in the branch of a tree overhanging the outside wall. I've just seen her climb up and hide one there myself!"

The headmistress could scarcely conceal her elation. "Show me where the note is hidden," she ordered, "and we'll set the wheels in motion at once to get her out of here!"

Together they reclaimed the note from the branch of the tree. The headmistress' hands trembled as she opened it. Then she hung her head and passed it silently to her assistant.

It read: "To whoever finds this — I love you!"

I don't think we realize how many very generous and understanding people there are in this country of ours. I told the story of this pathetic and unloved little orphan one morning on a popular radio show conducted by that superb lady Mary Margaret McBride, and although I stressed the point that it was fiction, with no basis whatever in fact, by noon the following day no fewer than nine wonderful people had called Miss McBride to say in effect, "What do we have to do to adopt that pathetic little kid Bennett Cerf told about? We'd like to give her just a little bit of the affection and understanding she's obviously never known in all her life — and see what it does for her."

SHORT BUT SWEET

There once lived a dog with such a high I.Q. that his owner sent him to college. Home for Christmas, the dog admitted he had learned neither history nor economics, but added proudly, "I *did* make rather a good start in foreign languages."

"Okay," conceded the owner. "Say something in a foreign language."

The dog said, "Meow."

* In the midst of a veritable downpour, a gallant driver saw a woman alone in the mud trying to change a flat tire, and couldn't bear passing her by. He completed the job for her, and, soaked to the skin, exclaimed jovially, "There, little lady, that's done!"

"Quiet," she ordered him. "You'll wake up my husband. He's taking a nap in the back seat."

* Mr. Horntoot admitted to his wife that he was feeling much better since his operation, but couldn't account for the enormous bump on the back of his head.

"Oh, that," chuckled Mrs. Horntoot. "Just before your operation they suddenly ran out of ether!"

* The wife of a submarine commander gave birth to a beautiful baby girl in the Norfolk Hospital while her husband's craft was patrolling Far Eastern waters. This is the cable she sent him: "Ahoy, skipper. New craft successfully launched at seven bells. Tonnage: eight pounds. No periscope. All shipshape. That is all, we hope. Love. Mary."

* Peter Lind Hayes tells about a magician who arrived at a millionaire's estate for a weekend, carrying a bag of props with his other luggage. A butler unpacked everything while the magician lunched, so when he went to his room he found in one drawer, impeccably laid out, three decks of marked cards, a stilleto, a collapsible bird cage, a revolver, and two sets of false teeth.

* A customer in a big department store asked the very Irish porter, "Do you know where the Chintz Room is?"

"That I do," he replied promptly, and pointed to a door labeled *Men*.

* A Purdue graduate returned home from his twenty-fifty class reunion in a very chastened mood. "My classmates," he told his wife sadly, "have all gotten so fat and bald they didn't recognize me."

* A millionaire manufacturer told his star salesman, "Marry one of my three daughters and I'll make you a full partner. Here are two of them. The third will be along any minute." The salesman, trained to make instantaneous decisions, snapped, "I'll take the one that's coming."

* On location, Raquel Welch took time off from her acting chores to go trout fishing. She hooked a whopper, but he finally broke loose and darted like all get-out to rejoin the other trout. "Wow, fellows," he boasted, expanding his gills, "you should have seen the one I got away from!"

* A Cleveland resident lost confidence in his cat, who spent his days snoozing unconcernedly in the sun while dozens of mice scurried happily by, so he bought a mousetrap. It's first victim was the cat.

* Anxious to get on in the world, a young couple was entertaining the boss and his wife at dinner — doing pretty well, too, until their young hopeful burst into view. He cased the boss's wife with obvious interest, then asked his dad, "Does she really wrestle on TV?"

* "Can you prove this is a good hair tonic?" an often-fooled baldheaded man asked his druggist, who answered, "One lady customer took the cork out of the bottle with her teeth and twenty-four hours later she had a mustache!"

* Intercepted correspondence between a boy and girl who sat next to each other in a third-grade class. Wrote the boy: "Dear Rosanne: I luv you. Do you luv me? Johnny." Answered the girl: "Dear Jonny: I do NOT love you. Love, Rosanne."

* The late Fred Allen claimed he found a New England seashore resort that was so dead the tide went out one day and refused to come back.

* A Texas oil magnate, getting his first look at the Eiffel Tower, conceded, "Right purty. How many barrels a day does it produce?"

* A seductive young siren from a nightclub chorus line suddenly added to her equipment a very big, very authentic, very expensive diamond ring.

"It *is* a beauty," she agreed with admiring cohorts, "but I'm afraid it carries the Slibovitz curse."

"That's one curse I never heard of," admitted the wardrobe mistress. "What is it?"

The siren eyed the ring sorrowfully and explained, "Slibovitz comes with it."

* Short-haired girl to long-haired lad, "Of course Daddy doesn't mind our being alone together every night. He thinks you're a girl!"

* A hopeful suitor dropped into a computer-dating center and registered his qualifications. He wanted someone who enjoyed water sports, liked company, favored formal attire, and was very small. The computer operated faultlessly. It sent him a penguin.

* A stranded Martian came upon two beautiful damsels in a nudist camp. He looked them over with obvious approval, then beseeched, "Take me to your tailor!"

* A well-known ham actor gave up Broadway and became a surgeon. One morning he removed an appendix so skillfully that several doctors watching him started to applaud. So he bowed gracefully and cut out the patient's gallbladder for an encore.

* A circus clown boasted that his brother had developed a new act never attempted before. He had himself shot out of a cannon four times as big as any used by previous stunt men.

"How did he stand the shock?" the clown was asked.

"That's hard to say," admitted the clown. "We never found him!"

* A bold ornithologist crossed a turkey with an ostrich, intent upon developing bigger drumsticks. The experiment, however, was a dismal failure. All he came up with was a scrawny bird who insisted on hiding his head in the mashed potatoes.

* After going the bachelor route for many long years, a successful manufacturer of men's hats met a girl who struck his fancy, wooed her, and won her. The day after the engagement was announced, the hatmaker danced delightedly about his office and cried to his partner, "Max, I've never been so happy! I'm on cloud seven and an eighth."

* Jack Benny swears that one evening when he was invited to play for the President, a guard stopped him outside the White House gate and asked, "Whatcha got in that case, Mr. Benny?"

Benny answered solemnly, "A machine gun."

With equal solemnity, the guard nodded. "Enter, friend. I was afraid for a minute it was your violin!"

* A new millionaire in Scarsdale was showing a friend around his modernistic "push-button" mansion. "Here's the best gadget of the lot," he exulted as they entered the master bedroom. "After a night out, I sometimes feel like stepping into a nice hot bath right here without the trouble of going into the bathroom. I just press this button . . ." He pressed the button and in rolled the bathtub, full of nice hot water — and the millionaire's wife.

* Have you heard about the tiger who cornered Mr. Aesop and ate him for Sunday dinner? "Well, Mr. Aesop," said the tiger as he finished his tasty repast. "I suppose you'll be making up a fable about *this* now, too!"

* The late Henry L. Mencken evolved a happy formula for answering all controversial letters. He simply replied, "Dear Sir (or Madam): You may be right!"

* A Georgetown crystal-gazer told a young client that something very amusing was to happen to her, then burst into uproarious laughter himself. The young lady arose and smacked his face.

"Why did you do that?" demanded the astonished clairvoyant.

"My mother," she said firmly, "always told me to strike a happy medium."

* A disgruntled movie actor nominates the aging head of a big studio as the politest gent in the world of the cinema and exhibits a telegram to prove it. It reads: "You're fired. Best regards."

* One of America's most popular socialites credits three simple words for making guests at her dinner parties feel welcome and at home. When they arrive, she murmurs, "At last!" and when they depart she protests, "Already?"

* An irate mother marched her ten-year-old son into a doctor's office and demanded, "Is a boy of this age able to perform an appendix operation?"

"Of course not," snapped the doctor.

Mama turned angrily on the boy and shouted, "So who was right? Put it back!"

* Item for the "Father of the Bride" department:

A delicate young wife-to-be sighed to her mother, "Oh dear, there are so many things to do before the wedding, and I don't want to overlook the most insignificant detail."

"Don't you worry your pretty little head," said the mother grimly. "I'll see that he's there!"

* "See what my friend sent me," boasted a beautiful receptionist. "An alligator purse, an alligator belt, and this lovely pair of alligator shoes."

"Your friend must be a philanthropist," said her sidekick.

"Not at all," replied the receptionist. "He's an alligator."

YOUNGER FRY

From the day your baby is born," counseled a famous scholar, "you must teach him to do without things. Children today love luxury too much. They have execrable manners, flaunt authority, have no respect for their elders. They no longer rise when their parents or teachers enter the room. What kind of awful creatures will they be when they grow up?"

The scholar who wrote these words, incidentally, was Socrates, shortly before his death in 399 B.C.

Farmer Ross had one of the finest apple orchards in the state, and come fall, regular as clockwork, the kids from the neighborhood would sneak in to purloin apples. Regularly, too, Farmer Ross would come charging angrily out of his house, waving a shotgun and threatening the fleeing youths with everything he could think of.

After watching these vain pursuits, a neighbor said to Farmer Ross, "Danged if I can understand you, Bill. You're normally a calm and generous man—and you've got ten times as many apples ripening in that orchard as you can possibly use. Why don't you just let the kids have some?"

"Heck," laughed Farmer Ross, "I *want* them to have the apples. But I was a boy once myself, and if I didn't holler and chase them—they'd never come back."

A small boy invaded the lingerie section a big department store and shyly presented his problem to a lady clerk. "I want to buy my mom a present of a slip," he said, "but I'm darned if I know what size she wears."

The clerk said, "It would help to know if your mom is tall or short, fat or skinny."

"She's just perfect," beamed the small boy, so the clerk wrapped up a size thirty-four for him.

Two days later Mom came to the store herself and changed it to a size fifty-two.

Eight-year-old Claudia was packed off to Waterbury for a visit with her old-maid aunt. Her last-minute instructions were, "Remember, Aunt Hester is a bit on the prissy side. If you have to go to the bathroom, be sure to say, 'I'd like to powder my nose.'"

Claudia made such a hit with Aunt Hester that when the time came for her to leave she was told, "I certainly loved having you here, my dear. On your next visit you must bring your little sister Sue with you."

"I better not," said Claudia hastily. "Sue still powders her nose in bed."

Mrs. Abernathy's eleven-year-old daughter, Nell, came home from camp with a gold medal for packing her trunk more neatly than any other girl.

"How did you do it," marveled Mrs. Abernathy, "when at home you can never clean up the mess you leave behind?"

"It was cinchy," explained Nell complacently. "I just never unpacked it all summer!"

A youngster devoted an entire rainy indoors afternoon to a drawing he was doing with varicolored crayons. His mother finally looked over his shoulder, and, puzzled, asked, "Who's that you're drawing, son?"

The son answered, "God."

"Don't be silly," reproved the mother. "Nobody knows what God looks like."

Not even pausing in his task, the son announced calmly, "They will when I'm finished!"

In a Philadelphia suburb there's a darling little seven-year-old daughter whose father likes to question her about her days in school. One evening the tot reported proudly, "This morning we started learning math-e-mat-ics. Did you study math-e-mat-ics when *you* went to school, Daddy?"

"I certainly did," he beamed. "How did you like it?"

"I loved it," she told him. "Isn't page five *good?*"

The annual Christmas playlet was the order of the day at a fashionable private school, and the coach chose an amiable, beautifully brought-up boy of seven to essay the role of the innkeeper at Bethlehem. He had trouble learning to turn away Mary and Joseph with a curt "There is no room at the inn," but had his part down pat by the end of the rehearsal period. Then came the big night, with his proud mother and father beaming at him from the first row of the orchestra. He boomed out his "There is no room at the inn" with great authority — but then he couldn't resist adding, "But come in, anyhow, and have some cookies and milk."

The son of a prominent film producer came home for his first vacation from college at the age of eighteen with a set of marks so glittering that the entire family glowed with pride. His five-year-old brother, nose slightly out of joint because of the adulation being poured upon the varsity prodigy, decided it was time to get into the act himself, and interrupted loudly, "I got an 'A' in arithmetic today."

His father replied indulgently, "I didn't know they taught arithmetic in kindergarten. What's one and one?"

The five-year-old pondered for a moment, then reported, "We haven't gotten that far yet."

A mischievous father wrote this letter to his beloved young daughter in summer camp:

Darling: Our home is fine. The food is okay and I like my wife. Yesterday we went on a trip to the golf course. The pro is nice and let me ride in a golf cart. I fed it some gasoline. Can I have a golf cart when you get home?

Today we had a competition downtown to see who could make money the fastest. I came in last. But your mother won the spending contest. Please send me a CARE package. Love, Dad.

Parents who came to watch their little darlings present a long-rehearsed historical pageant at a Massachusetts school one evening this spring got their biggest laugh from a climax that had not been planned. With Indians whooping it up outside a frontier stockade, three doughty soldiers clutched their bosoms, and holding their breath, made their death plunge to mats carefully laid out behind the scene.

Suddenly, however, the audience was astonished, to put it mildly, when the three bug-eyed soldiers suddenly reappeared in midair. A flint-hearted practical joker had replaced the mats with a trampoline.

"Willie," chided a ten-year-old lad's uncle, "isn't it about time you had a girl?"

"Golly, no," said Willie emphatically, and stomped off to have a catch.

The little girl from the house next door smiled to herself and said softly, "They're always the last ones to know!"

73

There lives on Lake Shore Drive a wealthy Chicagoan who has been brooding about his adored eight-year-old daughter, whose interest in life seems confined to just one subject: clothes. Arithmetic, history, and literature she disdains. All she does is pore over *Vogue, Harper's Bazaar, Women's Wear* and the fashion columns in the daily newspapers.

One evening recently she came home from her 1971 model school and casually reported that the class had been told the facts of life by an up-to-the-minute expert on sex.

"At last," exulted the father to himself, "my daughter has acquired a new interest." Eyes alight, he asked her, "Aren't there any questions at all about the things you heard today that you want to ask me?"

"Just one," replied the daughter promptly. "What does a girl *wear* for a thing like that?"

Young Jonathan had been promised a new puppy for his tenth birthday, but had a tough time choosing between a dozen likely candidates at the neighborhood pet shop.

Finally he decided upon one nondescript shaggy pup who was wagging his tail furiously.

Explained Jonathan, "I want the one with the happy ending."

A FEW OF MY FAVORITES

What can be more cheering than words of undying love from an innocent and beautiful young maiden? I quote a note received recently by a fortunate young friend of mine at Random House:

Dear Howard: I have been unable to sleep ever since I broke our engagement. Won't you forget and forgive? Your absence leaves a void nobody else can ever fill. I love you, I love you, I love you! Your adoring Susan.

P.S. Congratulations on winning the Irish Sweepstakes.

A sweet young thing toyed with the notion of signing up for a shorthand course.

"When we get finished with you," promised the enrollment clerk, "you'll be accurate, dependable, and neat."

"What about speed?" persisted the applicant.

"Our last nine graduates," said the enrollment clerk calmly, "married their bosses inside of five months."

A tired businessman came home one evening and said to his resolutely optimistic wife, "I've had a tough day at the office, so I'll welcome particularly this evening the good news you always have for me."

"It's better than ever tonight, darling," she burbled. "You know we have six children — and the wonderful news is that five of them didn't break an arm today."

When I addressed an audience of doctors San Diego, one of them assured me he was the hero of the story, widely circulated, about an operation on a bad-tempered old lady of eighty. She came through with flying colors despite all her dire prognostications, but set up a new clamor when the doctor told her that in accordance with the rules of the hospital, she'd have to walk ten minutes the very first day after her surgery and would have to get out entirely in a week, since beds there were at a premium.

Well, she had her ten-minute walk the first day, tottering but under her own steam, lengthened it to twenty minutes the second day, and by the time she went home, was stomping all over the hospital—including rooms where she had no right to be.

Later her family tried to pay the doctor a premium for his "wonderful job."

"Nonsense," he laughed. "It was just a routine operation."

"It's not the operation we're marveling over," said a grandson. "It's her walking. The old girl hadn't taken a step in six years!"

A Bostonian, whose business necessitated frequent trips to New York, divided his patronage among a half-dozen first-class midtown restaurants, but no matter what other delicacies were proferred on the menus, he invariably demanded a double order of snails.

"You have a one-track appetite when you come to New York," chided a friend. "Don't you have snails in Boston?"

"Of course we have," said the Bostonian, "but up there we don't seem able to catch them."

A certain distinguished gentleman from Arizona recently told an enthralled audience what happened when an apprehensive tenderfoot asked an old rancher, "What should I do if a rattlesnake bites me in the arm?"

"Get a friend to open the punctures the rattler made and suck the poison out for you," advised the rancher.

"And if I get bitten in the leg?"

"Follow the identical procedure," said the rancher.

"But suppose I'm unlucky enough to sit down on one of those darn rattlesnakes?"

"Ah, my boy," said the rancher solemnly, "that's the time you'll find out who your real friends are!"

An English lady, aboard an international train that originated in Switzerland, grew very fidgety as her train neared the border. She had struck up an acquaintance with a very friendly fellow passenger earlier in the journey, and now confided to him, "I mean to smuggle in this wristwatch I'm wearing, and I don't mind telling you I'm nervous as a cat about it."

A customs inspector marched into the compartment in due course and said, smiling, "I don't suppose either of you has failed to declare any dutiable objects."

Almost casually, the man pointed to the lady's watch and said, "I believe you'll find our friend here has overlooked that little bauble."

The watch was confiscated, while the lady dissolved into tears. When the train was in motion again, she demanded of her informer, "How could you be such a swine?"

The man pulled a valise out from under his seat and opened it, revealing a cache of at least a hundred brand-new, obviously expensive watches. "Don't take it so hard, lady," he advised. "Help yourself to any two of them!"

A stockbroker with very questionable ethics talked an uninitiated sucker into buying five thousand shares of a phony oil stock at fifty cents a share.

A week later the broker reported, "You're lucky! That stock has just doubled in price!"

"Buy me another five thousand," ordered the sucker.

A few days later the broker was on the phone again. "That stock's going wild!" he exulted. "It just hit two dollars a share!"

"That's enough for me," decided the sucker. "Sell all I've got at the market."

"*Sell?*" echoed the broker, stunned. "To *whom?*"

A famous big-game hunter was captured by African savages and imprisoned in a hut tastefully decorated with the shrunken, preserved heads of previous victims. A year later he managed to escape, however, and made his way to the nearest settlement, where he phoned his wife.

"I had given you up for lost," she sobbed.

"Never mind that," said the hunter. "Just rush me some new clothes. I'm in rags. I'll need a suit, size forty, a shirt, size sixteen, and some shoes, size ten-B. And oh yes," he added. "I'll need a hat, too. Size one."

The late Robert Sherwood, eminent playwright and wit, never quite knew how it had come about, but he found himself one day in a group of American tourists being herded through the Shakespeare country. The tour had reached Anne Hathaway's cottage in Stratford, and a painstaking guide was making a speech about every last object on the premises: "Here is the pot in which she brewed tea; here is the bureau on which she kept her knitting," etc.

The impatient Sherwood finally added an observation of his own: "And there is the chair in which she read her *London Times*. I can see her now the morning after *Hamlet* opened, scanning the review and muttering, 'Well, I guess the old so-and-so has another hit . . .' "

There is a fable about a very wise old man who was visited by a delegation of malcontents determined to tell him their troubles.

Suggested the wise man, "Write down your greatest trouble on a piece of paper." He then threw all the papers into a pot and said, "Now each of you draw a paper, and by all the laws of probability you will all have brand-new troubles to fret over."

The malcontents followed his suggestion. Then they read the new troubles they had been saddled with. The result: every single one of them clamored immediately to have his own trouble back!

There's a lady in the suburbs who is determined that when her twelve-year-old son Herbert grows up, he will be not only a Fred Astaire, but a Winston Churchill as well. With that end in view, she marches him to dancing school every Wednesday afternoon, and furthermore, sits grimly at the ringside to see that he not only pushes little girls around the room, more or less in tune with the music, but engages them in conversation at the same time. Herbert takes an exceedingly dim view of the entire procedure.

Last Wednesday, Herbert was executing what he fondly believed to be a foxtrot with a brand-new dancing partner when he caught his mother's signal: "Engage her in conversation!" He took a deep breath, and gallantly informed his lady fair, "Say, you sweat less than any fat girl I've ever danced with!"

Herbert won't have to go back to that dancing school for quite a spell.

Cleaning up his cluttered desk for the first time in months, a successful but careless businessman found wedged into a crack at the bottom of one of the drawers a redemption check for a pair of shoes he had left for repair way back in 1942—thirty years ago. The shop, he knew, still existed just around the corner, with the same sign on the outside: *Joe Antonio: Shoes Repaired While you Wait.* Joe was an artisan of the old school—a man who took intense pride in his work.

More or less as a joke, the businessman presented the check at Joe's, saying, "I know it's thirty years ago since I left these shoes here, but it occurred to me you just might be able to find them."

"Wait here. I go see," said the unsmiling Mr. Antonio. He handed back the check a moment later, explaining casually, "They'll be ready Tuesday."

There is an endless ritual—and highfalutin talk—in the selection of a proper wine and a proper vintage. Among connoisseurs, sending one bottle out of three back to the kitchen because it's "corky" or the wrong temperature is about par for the course.

There was one gourmet in Hollywood whose pretensions on the subject of wines became intolerable to his friends. To show him up, one of them went to extraordinary lengths. He searched the town for a bottle of the rarest and costliest French wine available, then poured its contents into an empty bottle of a cheap domestic brand advertised on TV at twenty-nine cents a quart. Then he asked the gourmet for dinner.

The mere sight of the twenty-nine-cent bottle made the gourmet turn pale, and when his glass was filled he looked wildly for the nearest exit. There was no escape, however, so, with the host and his wife watching intently, he took one small sip. Then he took another.

His reputation hung in the balance. He

was equal to the test. He put down his glass very gently, smacked his lips, and said, "My dear boy, you never should have tried a juvenile trick like this. *You can't afford it!*"

A partially deaf gentleman was extolling the virtues of his new hearing aid. "It's marvelous," he enthused to a friend. "Since I acquired it, I now can hear the birds singing in the trees and the crickets chirping on the hearth. I can also hear clearly a conversation being conducted in an apartment a full block away!"

"You don't say," said his friend. "What kind is it?"

The proud owner consulted his wristwatch and answered, "Twenty minutes after two."

Gal from a local editorial office—the athletic type—went up to a highly publicized ski lodge for a weekend of risking life and limb on the glistening slopes. The morning after her arrival she complained to the manager that twice during the night she had to get dressed and go to the lobby for a carafe of ice water.

"My dear young lady," said the manager, "why didn't you simply press the buzzer beside your bed?"

"The buzzer?" exclaimed the girl. "The bellboy told me that was the fire alarm!"

An ingenious dentist found a way to handle a particularly nervous lady patient. She panicked regularly the moment she seated herself in his chair, and clamped her mouth so tightly that he couldn't pry it open. So one afternoon he had his girl assistant sneak up behind her, and as soon as he was ready to drill, she got the signal to jab the lady in the rear with a hatpin. She opened her mouth to holler — and that was that.

His ministrations completed, the dentist consoled the patient, "Now, that wasn't so bad after all, was it?"

"Not quite," she admitted, still trembling, "but I certainly didn't expect to feel the pain so far down!"

From a rural district of England comes the story of a driver of a small sedan braking hastily as the tweedy mistress of the largest estate nearby came hurtling around a sharp bend in the narrow road in her large Rolls. Before he could say a word, she shouted *"Pig!"* and drove on.

"Fat old cow," he cried after her in retaliation. Then he drove round the bend himself—and crashed head-on into the biggest pig he had ever seen.

The heroes of this story are two gray-haired Middle European playwrights who have loathed and been insanely jealous of each other for years, but who embrace each other fervently and express undying love and admiration every time they meet. At one of these meetings Playwright One reminisced, "The crowning night of my life, I guess, came when my new drama opened during World War Two, and the first-night audience stood and cheered me for a full hour after the final curtain fell. Did you happen to be there, my dear friend?"

"No," answered Playwright Two reflectively. "Fortunately, at the time, I was in a concentration camp."

The gentle art of press agentry goes all the way back to the days of the Old Testament — if this story can be believed. It seems that Moses' crack publicity man — on the edge of the Red Sea — urged him to build a bridge across so his people could escape the wrath of the Egyptians.

"We haven't time for that," demurred Moses. "Instead, I figure I'll order the Red Sea to part and just lead my folks across. How does that notion strike you?"

The press agent, visibly impressed, told Moses, "You do that, Moses, and I'll guarantee you at least two full pages in the Old Testament."

A draftee was assigned as a chauffeur to a colonel who had a keen eye for a pretty girl. One afternoon the colonel spotted a real beauty ankling along Park Avenue in the opposite direction, and ordered the chauffeur, "Turn the car around on the double and pull up alongside that young lady."

The driver promptly stalled his motor in carrying out the directive, and by the time he got it going again, the beauty had disappeared in the crowd.

"Soldier," snapped the irritated colonel, "you'd be a total loss in an emergency."

"I think you're wrong, sir," hazarded the soldier. "That was *my* girl."

Two friends motored home from a fishing trip in Maine. On a lonely country road they encountered engine trouble. Who answered their knock at the nearest farmhouse? Right! The farmer's beautiful daughter. She gave them dinner and let them stay overnight. Six months later one of the friends received an ominous-looking document. A frown disappeared as he read it, and then he phoned his fishing companion.

"I say, Tom," he said. "Did you by any chance spend a little time with that beautiful farm girl the night our car broke down?"

"Why, yes," answered Tom sheepishly.

"And did you, in a moment of Machiavellian cunning, give her my name and address?"

"Now, don't get sore about that," broke in Tom. "Where's your sense of humor?"

"Oh, I'm not a bit sore," his friend assured him. "I just thought you'd like to know I heard from her lawyer. She died last week and left me the farm and twelve thousand dollars in cash."

A rich but well-seasoned old maid in Philadelphia finally landed an eligible gent. She was dreadfully near-sighted, but knowing how much stock he put in perfect physical health, was resolved to conceal this defect from him by hook or crook. One day she surreptitiously fastened a diamond stickpin into a tree, and later, seated with her swain on a bend two hundred yards away, exclaimed, "Look, darling! Isn't that a diamond sparkling in yonder oak tree?"
her swain on a bench two hundred yards away, exclaimed, "Look, darling! Isn't that a diamond sparkling in yonder oak tree?"

"I'm sure I couldn't see a diamond as far away as that."

"I'll get it for you," she said happily, and got up to retrieve it. Suddenly her house of cards collapsed. She tripped over a cow.

In the time of Nero, when sport-loving Romans crowded the Colosseum every Saturday to see a Christian tossed to the lions (on some Sundays there were double-headers), there was one special victim who had given the authorities untold trouble before he was rounded up. Nero had eleven of his most ferocious lions starved for a full week to assure a neat performance when they were turned on this Christian the following Saturday. Eighty thousand spectators turned out, not including the press. The Christian stood alone in the center of the arena, calm and unafraid.

The first lion was released. He made a beeline for the Christian. The crowd wetted its lips. But then an amazing thing happened. The Christian bent down and whispered something in the lion's ear. The lion's tail went between his legs, he lowered his head and slinked out of the arena.

When the same performance was followed by six more half-starved kings of the forest, and the gallant crowd was beginning to holler for its money back,

100

Nero, sore as a pup, summoned the Christian and curtly said, "If you will tell me what you say to those lions to make them act that way, I will grant you a full pardon."

"It's very simple, Nero," explained the Christian. "I just whisper in their ears: 'Remember, you'll be expected to say a few words after dinner!' "

A wealthy lady who had a big estate in Westchester met an old friend on a train bound for Mt. Kisco, but simply couldn't remember her name. The conversation is bound to give me a clue, she thought, but for a half-hour she got nowhere.

Then the friend said, "My poor brother is working himself to death these days."

The lady felt that her moment had come. "Ah yes, your dear brother," she exclaimed. "And what is he doing now?"

Her companion glared. "He is still President of the United States," she remarked coldly.

The UN delegate from a tiny new state deep in the African jungle was without question the most magnificent physical specimen reporters at Kennedy Airport had ever seen.

"How do you keep in such marvelous condition? Is it the diet you adhere to?" asked an admiring girl newshawk.

"I just eat beans," shrugged the towering delegate.

"Just beans!" echoed the girl. "That's amazing! You mean navy beans? Regular beans? Soy beans?"

"No, no," corrected the delegate. *"Human* bein's!"

Young Dr. Anderson hung out his shingle for the first time on a Tuesday, but no patient showed up until Friday morning. When the man came into his office, Dr. Anderson thought it advisable to impress him. He picked up his telephone and barked into it, "I have so many patients scheduled to visit me today that I am afraid I won't be able to get over to the hospital to perform that brain operation until six this evening." He banged up the receiver and turned to his visitor with a disarming smile. "What seems to be paining you, my good man?" he said.

"Nothing is paining me," said the bewildered visitor. "I have just come to hook up your phone, sir."

A favorite picture star, who married well—and often—found it expedient to get a divorce in a hurry a few months ago. Her lawyer suggested Mexico.

"But I don't speak Spanish," she protested.

"That's all right," said the lawyer. "Whenever there's a pause, all you have to do is say *si, si.*"

The star created a great sensation in the little Mexican village, and when she appeared in court, the whole town turned out to witness the event. There was a great deal of emoting and bowing, and the star said *"si, si"* very firmly on numerous occasions. Suddenly the crowd gave a great cheer. "Well, I guess I'm divorced," she said complacently.

"Divorced, my eye," cried the perspiring attorney. "You've married the mayor!"

This is an era of violent change, of insecurity, and crass materialism, but an old fable that I found in a volume of folklore of the Near East emphasizes the fact that there are two things that remain about the same in every century and every clime: the heart and mother love.

This fable tells of a spoiled, willful son in ancient Judea who came to his mother and declared, "I have fallen in love with a maid of surpassing beauty, but she trusts not my protestations. 'If you really love me,' says she, 'you will cut out your mother's heart and place it before me on a golden tray.'"

The mother gazed deep into the eyes of her son, then unhesitatingly bared her breast. And the son cut out her heart.

In mad haste, he dashed with it toward the home of his beloved. When he stumbled over the root of a tree, the heart, bleeding, called out softly, "Be careful, son of mine. If you run so fast, you may fall and hurt yourself."

An old Jewish peddler ambled down a street in Tel Aviv carrying two large watermelons. A tourist stopped him to ask, "Where is Ben Yehuda Street?"

The peddler answered, "Please hold these two watermelons."

The tourist managed to gather them in his arms, whereupon the peddler made an expansive gesture with his hands and exclaimed petulantly, "How should I know?"

One summer evening, just before dark, a man was driving his wife along a lonely country road when she suddenly complained of a violent headache. One look at her agonized expression convinced him that something was radically wrong. He remembered that about ten miles back, he had passed a little cottage with a doctor's shingle on the gate. He turned the car about in a pasture and drove to the doctor's house as quickly as he dared.

A gray-haired, white-jacketed little man with sharp, twinkling eyes answered his summons. He took one look at the ailing wife, and said simply, "Carry her into my office at once." The man waited impatiently while the doctor made a cursory examination, then followed him into his anteroom when bidden. "Something is pressing on your wife's brain," said the doctor. "I'm afraid she must be operated upon immediately. If you wait even until you get her back to town it probably will be too late." The man gasped. "I'm willing to perform the operation," continued the doctor, "but I'm all alone in the house and you will have to help me. I'll do my best, but won't answer for the consequences."

There was something in the doctor's manner that inspired confidence. Besides, the woman's condition was obviously desperate. "Go ahead," said the man grimly.

The operation had reached its most delicate stage when the man became aware of an insistent banging on the front door. As soon as he could, he went to throw it open, and found two uniformed men waiting to enter. One of them had a gun under his arm. "The little doctor slipped away from us again," he said. "We usually find him pottering around here."

"Who are you?" asked the man.

"Guards at the asylum over the hill," was the answer. "Where's the doctor? Got to get him back before he gets violent!"

"Good God!" said the main. "He's in the middle of an operation on my wife's brain. You'll have to let him finish. Get me an ambulance—quick!"

Fifteen minutes later the doctor came out of the parlor and declared the operation completed. The ambulance from the asylum was already at the door. One attendant helped the man lift his wife gently into the back, while the other led the unprotesting doctor away.

The ride back to New York was a nightmare for the distraught man. His wife had not regained consciousness when he arrived at the home of his own private physician on Park Avenue. "Be quick," he begged. "Something terrible has happened to her. Tell me if anything can be done before it is too late."

It was a sorely puzzled man who came to him a short while later. "This case baffles me completely," the doctor said. "Your wife will live. She has been saved by an almost miraculous operation. But this is the factor that stops me cold. I know of only one man in this world who has the skill and the knowledge to perform an operation of this character. And that man has been in an insane asylum for the past six years!"

Along about 1960 a reporter from the *London Standard* demanded of Sir Winston Churchill, "What do you say, sir, to the prediction that in the year 2000, women will be ruling the entire world?"

Sir Winston raised a quizzical eyebrow and murmured, "They still will, eh?"

Winning a battle with a computer is getting to be more fun than sneaking into the subway through an exit gate used to be when we were kids. Let's give a great big hand to latest winner, Jerome T. Parker. Mr. Parker, for reasons unknown to him, received a bill from an oil company for several consecutive months for $0.00. He laughingly showed the bills to friends and waited for the bills to stop coming. When he got one marked *Final Notice,* however, plus a threat to turn the account over to a notoriously tough collection agency, he wrote out a check for no dollars and no cents, signed his name thereto, and mailed it to the oil company with a note saying, "This pays my account in full."

Darned if he didn't get a form letter in return thanking him for his patronage.

A recent Mayor of New York City, with a campaign for re-election in the offing, initiated a big clean-up drive. One of his stunts was to set up a special trash can in Times Square and wire it for sound. A small transmitter-receiver was hidden in the can, while an operator with a mike was stationed in a window overlooking the square.

Several intrigued reporters were watching when a lady threw an old newspaper on the sidewalk. The trash can admonished her, "That's not the way to keep New York clean, lady. What's your name?"

The lady shot one startled look at the can, then snapped, "I don't talk to trash cans"—and strode away.

There was a resourceful radio announcer who arranged to do a broadcast from the city dog pound. As listeners heard a cacophony of mournful barking by stray pooches, they were told that if they contributed just one dollar to the cause, they would not only save one otherwise doomed animal's life, they would be presented with the dog as well.

A week later the ecstatic director of the dog pound called up the announcer to tell him, "What a sensational hit that broadcast of yours made. The dollar bills have been pouring in so fast I've had to hire three extra dog catchers to fill the orders."

The late John Mason Brown, Kentucky's gift to women's clubs the country over, had just completed one of his witty, polished lectures when one little white-haired lady, leaning heavily on her cane, approached the podium to tell him, "I've taken the liberty to speak to you, sir, because you said you loved old ladies."

"Indeed I do," said that super-diplomat Brown, "but I also love them your age, my dear."

Two Irish upstairs maids had the same day off—and had the time of their lives boasting of the ways they bamboozled their exacting employers. "Here's a new trick I just picked up," chortled one. "The lady I work for is always reminding me I must warm the plates for all the dinner guests, but that's too darn much work. So I just warm hers—and she never knows the difference!"

A famous movie star whose name had been coupled for romantic interludes with every beauty in Hollywood entered a Long Island hospital for a check-up and was fawned upon and babied by every nurse in the institution. One particularly attractive nurse was at his side, it seemed, every time he stirred. When he finally indicated that he'd like to be alone for just a little while, she told him, "Now if you want anything at all, you need only pull this cord."

He gave her his patented irresistible smile and said, "Thank you, my dear. What is the cord attached to?"

She smiled back and answered, "Me."

ABOUT THE AUTHOR

Bennett Cerf was born in New York City and educated at Columbia University, from which he received his B.A. in 1919 and 1920 his Litt.B. from the School of Journalism. After a short period as a reporter on the *New York Herald Tribune,* and a little longer stretch in a Wall Street brokerage house, he became a vice-president of the publishing house Boni and Liveright.

In 1925 Bennett Cerf and Donald Klopfer, his friend since childhood, bought from Boni and Liveright the Modern Library, and in 1927 the two young publishers decided to publish "at random" general trade books. Among the writers who would later be published by the newly established Random House were William Faulkner, John O'Hara, Eugene O'Neill, Robert Penn Warren, James Michener, Isak Dinesen, Truman Capote and many others. There was one best-selling author, however, who until this book never appeared on the Random House list—Bennett Cerf, although he wrote and edited over seventeen books on humor published by other companies.

Bennett Cerf was well known for his syndicated newspaper column, his appearances as a regular panelist on the television program *What's My Line?* and as a popular lecturer, but most of all he was known as a great publisher. With his wife, Phyllis, and their two sons, Jonathan and Christopher, Mr. Cerf spent most of his time at his houses in New York and Mount Kisco, where he died in August, 1971, at the age of seventy-three.